Made in the USA
Monee, IL
10 March 2022

92645785R10069